READY, SET, DRAW!
FAIRIES AND PRINCESSES

AILIN CHAMBERS

 Gareth Stevens
PUBLISHING

Please visit our website, **www.garethstevens.com**. For a free color catalog of all our high-quality books, call toll free 1-800-542-2595 or fax 1-877-542-2596.

Library of Congress Cataloging-in-Publication Data

Chambers, Ailin.
Fairies and Princesses / by Ailin Chambers.
p. cm. — (Ready, set, draw!)
Includes index.
ISBN 978-1-4824-0931-4 (pbk.)
ISBN 978-1-4824-0916-1 (6-pack)
ISBN 978-1-4824-0915-4 (library binding)
1. Fairies in art — Juvenile literature. 2. Princesses in art — Juvenile literature. 3. Drawing — Technique — Juvenile literature. I. Chambers, Ailin. II. Title.
NC825.F22 C43 2015
743.4—d23

First Edition

Published in 2015 by
Gareth Stevens Publishing
111 East 14th Street, Suite 349
New York, NY 10003

Editors: Samantha Hilton, Kate Overy and Joe Harris
Illustrations: Dynamo Limited
Design concept: Keith Williams
Design: Dynamo Limited and Notion Design
Cover design: Ian Winton

Printed in the United States of America

CPSIA compliance information: Batch #CS15GS: For further information contact Gareth Stevens, New York, New York at 1-800-542-2595.

CONTENTS

WOOD FAIRY

FAIRYTALE PRINCESS

SKY FAIRY

PIRATE PRINCESS

FLAME FAIRY

NATIVE AMERICAN PRINCESS

EXPLORER FAIRY

AFRICAN PRINCESS

FAIRY GODMOTHER

ARABIAN PRINCESS

RAINBOW FAIRY

GRAB THESE!

Are you ready to create some amazing pictures? Wait a minute! Before you begin drawing, you will need a few important pieces of equipment.

PENCILS

You can use a variety of drawing tools, such as pens, chalks, pencils, and paints. But to begin use an ordinary pencil.

PAPER

Use a clean sheet of paper for your final drawings. Scrap paper is useful and cheap for your practice work.

ERASERS

Everyone makes mistakes! That's why every artist has a good eraser. When you erase a mistake, do it gently. Erasing too hard will ruin your drawing and possibly even rip it.

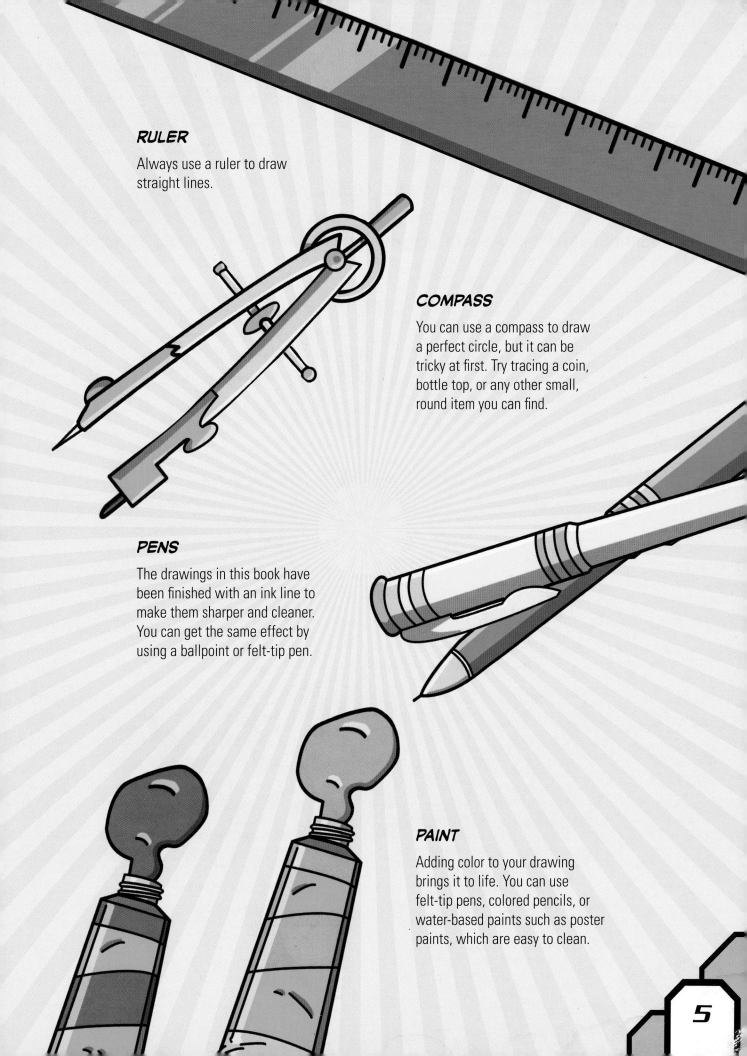

RULER

Always use a ruler to draw straight lines.

COMPASS

You can use a compass to draw a perfect circle, but it can be tricky at first. Try tracing a coin, bottle top, or any other small, round item you can find.

PENS

The drawings in this book have been finished with an ink line to make them sharper and cleaner. You can get the same effect by using a ballpoint or felt-tip pen.

PAINT

Adding color to your drawing brings it to life. You can use felt-tip pens, colored pencils, or water-based paints such as poster paints, which are easy to clean.

GETTING STARTED

In this book, we use a simple two–color system to show you how to draw a picture. Just remember: New lines are blue lines!

STARTING WITH STEP 1

The first lines you will draw are very simple shapes. They will be shown in blue. You should draw them with a normal pencil.

ADDING MORE DETAIL

As you move on to the next step, the lines you have already drawn will be shown in black. The new lines for that step will appear in blue.

FINISHING YOUR PICTURE

When you reach the final stage, you will see the image in full color with a black ink line. Inking a picture means tracing the main lines with a black pen. After the ink dries, use your eraser to remove all the pencil lines before adding your color.

EXPERT COLORING

LIGHT AND SHADE

If you want to make your picture look 3-D, start thinking about light and shade. Decide which side of your picture is in shadow, and make the colors darker along either the left or right edge. Just use a darker version of the color you have already used in that area.

FELT-TIP PENS

You can create bold colors and strong lines with felt-tip pens. However, it's not easy to correct mistakes that you've made with a pen. So start off with a pencil sketch first! Add the felt-tip colors once you're happy with the result.

COLORED PENCILS

These create a lighter and less dramatic look than felt-tips. Colored pencils are also easier to blend together. Sketch your drawing first with a pencil. Then, gently layer your color, making it as light or as dark as you like.

WATERCOLORS

Watercolors are easy to blend together. First, sketch your drawing with a waterproof pen. Then, add water to your paint, but don't add too much. If you do, it might ruin your paper.

WOOD FAIRY

A wood fairy is a mischievous fairy. She has pointy ears like an elf and delicate wings that help her flutter from tree to tree.

STEP 1

First, draw the shape above to make the fairy's body.

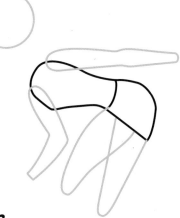

STEP 2

Next, add arms, legs, and a simple circle to start the fairy's head.

STEP 3

Draw a pointed shape on the circle for her chin. Carefully draw her hands, and add her lower legs.

STEP 4

Now, add her hair, a pointy ear, a neck, and her feet. Her hair can be any style, including this pixie cut.

STEP 5

After adding her clothes and face, draw her fairy wings.

STEP 6

You can make your fairy any color you want. Just remember that she has to look at home among flowers and trees.

FAIRYTALE PRINCESS

This fairytale princess wears a long, flowing gown and a golden crown. She looks happy, and her dress sparkles as if it's been sprinkled with fairy dust.

STEP 1

First, draw a stylish dress that curves out at the bottom.

STEP 2

Add a circle for her head and long, slender arms.

STEP 3

Carefully draw her hands, and add a pointed chin.

STEP 4

Add her feet, a big bow, puffy sleeves, more details, and her crown. Draw her hair, ear, and neck. Add the little bird sitting on her finger.

STEP 5

Finish her face, her shoes, and the little bird. Then, add more details to her dress.

STEP 6

It's time to add color! We've chosen blue, but you could use any color.

SUPER TIP!

An easy way to add sparkle to the princess's dress is to leave small dots without color.

Another way to make the small, white sparkles is to add little dots of white poster paint.

Don't bunch the dots up in one place.

SKY FAIRY

Sky fairies spend their days playing hide–and–seek in the clouds. These fairies have soft, rounded wings, and they even look a bit like fluffy clouds.

STEP 1

First, draw two shapes in a way that looks like a lowercase *i*.

STEP 2

Add her arms, chin, and her cloud skirt.

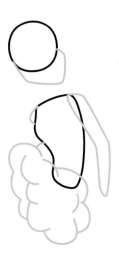

STEP 3

Carefully add her hand and the top of her legs.

STEP 4

Finish off her legs, then draw her mouth and ear. Add a big, fluffy hairstyle that looks like cotton candy!

STEP 5

Now, add her eyes and her other hand. Soft, rounded wings complete the picture.

SUPER TIP!

It's very easy to change the sky fairy into a storm fairy by changing the colors of her clothes, hair, and face.

We've used dark blue and purple to make her a storm fairy. You can use other colors to make her into another type of fairy!

STEP 6

Your fairy could be a bright sky fairy like this one. Or you could use darker colors to make her a storm fairy.

13

PIRATE PRINCESS

This pirate princess may not wear a long dress, but her golden crown and purple clothes show that she's real royalty!

STEP 1

Draw the pirate princess's main body shape, which is shown here.

STEP 2

Add her head and the tops of her arms and legs.

STEP 3

Draw her arms, hands, and lower legs. Then, add her chin and a line across her forehead for her crown.

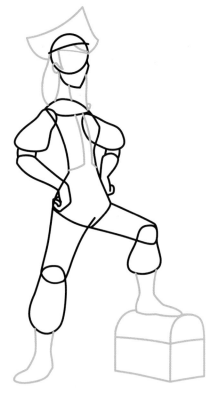

STEP 4

Add chunky pirate boots and a pointed pirate hat. Don't forget her chest of precious jewels.

STEP 5

Add her waistcoat, crown, belt, and hoop earrings. Give the treasure chest more detail. An eye patch completes her look!

STEP 6

Color her in with bold colors. We've used purple, but you can use any of your favorite colors. Make her crown look shiny.

FLAME FAIRY

Bright red hair, flaming wings, and an orange dress tell you that this fairy is hot stuff. She really looks like she's made of fire!

STEP 1

First, draw the top of her dress and then add her fire skirt. Use pointy shapes to make it look like it's moving.

STEP 2

Next, add a circle for her head. Then, draw her long arms and the top parts of her legs.

STEP 3

Now, add her pointy chin and one hand. Finish her legs.

STEP 4

Add her ears, flaming hair, wings, and pointy feet.

STEP 5

Now, draw her face, and add
some simple lines
for her dress and shoes.

STEP 6

Choose colors such as orange
and red to make a flame fairy.
Use shades of blue and white if
you want to make an ice fairy.

NATIVE AMERICAN PRINCESS

This Native American princess wears her traditional dress with pride. Decorate her outfit with plenty of tassels and feathers.

STEP 1

First, draw these shapes to make her body.

STEP 2

Next, add a circle for her head. Draw her arms and the tops of her legs.

STEP 3

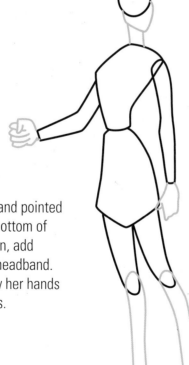

Draw a tilted and pointed shape at the bottom of the circle. Then, add her neck and headband. Carefully draw her hands and lower legs.

STEP 4

Add the staff, hair, cuffs and feet. Also, add more details to her dress.

STEP 5

Draw feathers on her staff and her headband. Add lots of fringe to her dress. Finish her face and shoes.

STEP 6

Her clothes are made from animal skins, but you could also decorate them with drawings of jewels.

AFRICAN PRINCESS

This African princess's dress may look simple, but its bright colors, her pretty jewels, and her feathered headband make her look truly royal.

STEP 1

Start by drawing her long dress to make a simple body shape.

STEP 2

Now, add her head, long neck, and arms to give her a royal look.

STEP 3

Add her pointed chin, her hands, and her bare feet.

STEP 4

Draw her pretty headband with its feathers. Add her earrings, cuffs, and a fold in her dress.

STEP 5

Now draw her face and necklace, and add stripes to her dress.

STEP 6

Use bright colors to help this princess pop off the page!

FAIRY GODMOTHER

A fairy godmother is always ready to help people. She'll use her fairy wings and magic wand to sort out any problem.

STEP 1

Use these two round shapes to begin drawing her body.

STEP 2

Add a circle for her head, and draw her arms.

STEP 3

Draw her hair and face. Her hands and little legs come next.

STEP 4

She needs some fairy wings, so she can fly. Don't forget her magic wand!

STEP 5

Finish her face. Then, top the wand with a magic star, and add a shawl over her shoulders.

STEP 6

Choose friendly, bold colors for your fairy godmother. You can always add some sparkles, too.

SUPER TIP!

Add some sparkles to your fairy's magic wand to show how magical it is.

- A very simple way to make sparkles is to draw a small group of shapes like these circles and stars.

  ✳ ○

- Draw the shapes around the wand. Some of them can trail behind the wand to show how it's moving.

ARABIAN PRINCESS

This Arabian princess looks fabulous in her pink two-piece outfit and sparkling jewels. She's ready to take a trip on a magic carpet!

STEP 1

First, draw a simple body shape made up of pants and a top.

STEP 2

Next, add an oval shape for her head. Then, draw her arms and feet.

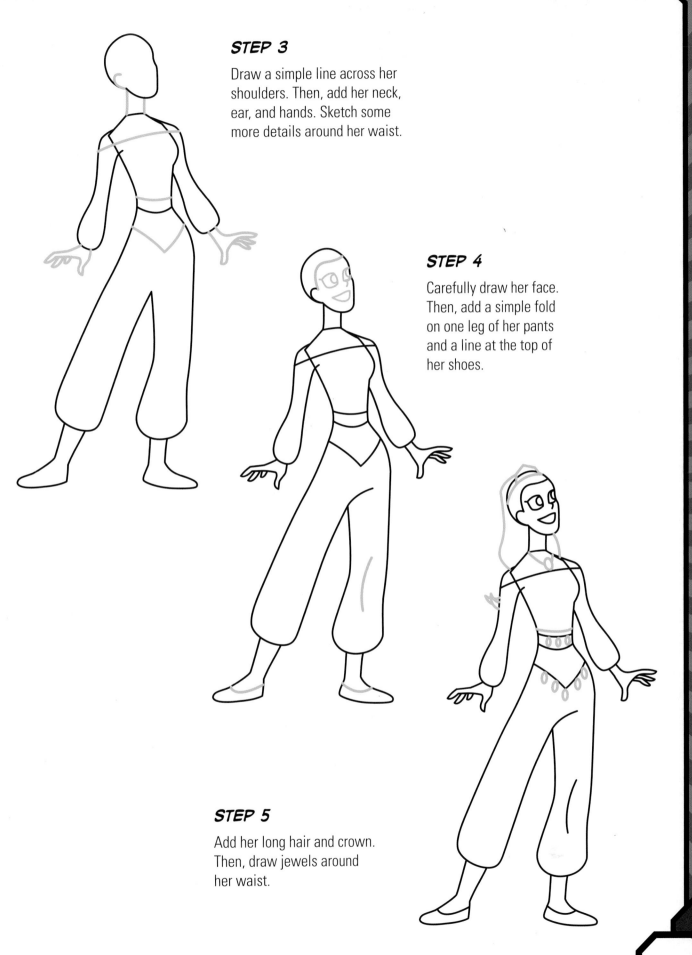

STEP 3

Draw a simple line across her shoulders. Then, add her neck, ear, and hands. Sketch some more details around her waist.

STEP 4

Carefully draw her face. Then, add a simple fold on one leg of her pants and a line at the top of her shoes.

STEP 5

Add her long hair and crown. Then, draw jewels around her waist.

STEP 6

We've colored her
outfit in shades of
pink. You could even
add a magic carpet!

This fairy loves bright colors. Her skirt is like a beautiful rainbow. With a wave of her magic wand, she paints across the sky.

STEP 1

First, draw a simple shape for her curved skirt and top.

STEP 2

Next, draw her head, which should be slightly tilted. Draw a bent leg, a straight leg, and her arms.

STEP 3

Now, sketch
her wings, and
carefully draw her
hands.

STEP 4

Add feet, hair,
dress details, and
a magic wand.

STEP 5

Now, finish her face. Then, add the rainbow. You could trace around a cup to get the curve just right.

STEP 6

It's time to color! Remember, she's a rainbow fairy, so use as many different colors as possible!

GLOSSARY

10-14

3-D Three-dimensional. An object that has height, width, and depth, like an object in the real world.

chunky Heavy and thick.

cuff The end part of a sleeve, around the wrist.

elf A creature from folk tales with pointed ears and magical powers.

pixie A mischievous, playful elf or fairy.

poster paint A water-based, bright-colored paint often used for posters.

tassel A bunch of loose threads that are bound at one end and used as a decoration on curtains or clothes.

watercolor An artist's paint that is thinned with water to give it a transparent quality.

FURTHER READING

How to Draw Fairies by David Antram (Bookhouse, 2011)

How to Draw Fairies and Mermaids by Fiona Watt (Usborne Publishing, 2013)

WEBSITES

fairytownlove.weebly.com/index.html

www.disney.co.uk/disney–fairies/games

www.educationalcoloringpages.com/fairy.html

INDEX